Beautiful Names for a Beautiful Baby

By Jane Summers

<u>A</u>

Aadam
Aadhya
Aadil
Aadya
Aahana
Aahil
Aaleyah
Aaliyah
Aanya
Aarav
Aariz
Aarna
Aarohi
Aaron
Aarush
Aarya
Aaryan
Aavya
Aayan
Aayush
Abalone
Abbas
Abbey

Abbie
Abbigail
Abby
Abbygail
Abdiel
Abdirahman
Abdul
Abdullah
Abdullahi
Abdulrahman
Abdur
Abdurrahman
Abe
Abel
Abelard
Abelia
Aberforth
Abigail
Abigale
Abilene
Abina
Abner
Abraham
Abram
Abriella
Abrielle
Abril

Abu	Adalynn
Abubakar	Adalynne
Abygail	Adam
Acacia	Adamaris
Acacio	Adan
Acacius	Addalyn
Acadia	Addax
Acantha	Addelyn
Ace	Addilyn
Acedia	Addilynn
Acer	Addison
Achilles	Addisyn
Acker	Addyson
Ackley	Adela
Acton	Adelaida
Ada	Adelaide
Adair	Adelard
Adalardo	Adelbert
Adalee	Adele
Adalia	Adelia
Adalie	Adelin
Adalina	Adelina
Adalind	Adeline
Adaline	Adelio
Adaly	Adelle
Adalyn	Adelyn
Adalyne	Adelyne

Adelynn
Adelynne
Adem
Aden
Aderyn
Adesina
Adetokunbo
Adger
Adhya
Adia
Adil
Adilene
Adin
Adina
Adira
Aditi
Aditya
Adlai
Adler
Adley
Admon
Adnan
Adolfo
Adolph
Adonis
Adrian
Adriana

Adrianna
Adriano
Adriatic
Adriel
Adrien
Adrienne
Advika
Adyan
Adyn
Aegle
Aella
Aeneas
Aengus
Aeon
Aerin
Aeris
Aerith
Aero
Aerolynn
Aeson
Afia
Afonso
Afric
Africa
Afsaneh
Afsha
Afton

Agamemnon	Ailany
Agatha	Ailbhe
Agathon	Ailee
Aglaia	Aileen
Aglaze	Ailidh
Agnes	Ailill
Agrippina	Ailis
Agrona	Ailsa
Agustin	Ailyn
Ahana	Aimee
Ahearn	Aimi
Ahern	Aimilios
Ahmad	Aina
Ahmed	Aine
Ahmir	Aingeal
Ai	Ainhoa
Aida	Ainsley
Aidan	Aira
Aiden	Airell
Aidric	Airic
Aife	Airyck
Aigneis	Aisha
Aika	Aislinn
Aiken	Aislynn
Aiko	Aitana
Aila	Aithne
Ailani	Aiya

Aiyana	Alameda
Aiyanna	Alamo
Aiza	Alan
Ajax	Alana
Ajay	Alanah
Akako	Alane
Akane	Alani
Akasuki	Alanna
Akela	Alannah
Akemi	Alanson
Aki	Alaric
Akihiko	Alastair
Akihiro	Alastrina
Akiko	Alastrine
Akina	Alastriona
Akira	Alaya
Akita	Alayah
Aksel	Alayla
Akshara	Alayna
Al	Alba
Alaa	Albedo
Alabaster	Alberic
Aladdin	Albert
Alaia	Alberta
Alain	Alberto
Alaina	Albie
Alaiya	Albina

Albion
Albus
Alby
Alcaeus
Alcott
Alda
Alden
Alder
Aldo
Aldric
Aldrich
Aleah
Alec
Aled
Aleeah
Aleen
Aleena
Aleenah
Aleia
Alejandra
Alejandro
Aleksander
Aleksandra
Aleksandrina
Alena
Alene
Aleph

Aleron
Alessa
Alessandra
Alessandro
Alessia
Alessio
Alethea
Aletris
Alex
Alexa
Alexander
Alexandra
Alexandre
Alexandria
Alexandru
Alexi
Alexia
Alexis
Alexsus
Alexxa
Alexzander
Aleyah
Aleyda
Aleydis
Aleyna
Aleyza
Alfie

Alfie-james
Alfie-lee
Alfonso
Alford
Alfred
Alfredo
Algernon
Ali
Alia
Aliah
Aliana
Alianna
Alibeth
Alice
Alicia
Alienor
Alijah
Alima
Alina
Alinah
Aline
Alinna
Alisa
Alisha
Alison
Alissa
Alisson

Alistair
Alivia
Aliya
Aliyah
Aliyana
Aliza
Alizae
Alizah
Alizay
Alize
Allan
Allard
Allegra
Allen
Allena
Allene
Allie
Allison
Allisson
Allston
Allura
Ally
Allyn
Allyson
Alma
Almeda
Almera

Almond	Alvina
Aloe	Alviria
Alohi	Alwyn
Alois	Alya
Alok	Alyah
Alon	Alyana
Alondra	Alyanna
Alonso	Alycia
Alonzo	Alyna
Alora	Alynna
Aloysius	Alys
Alpha	Alyson
Alphaeus	Alyssa
Alpine	Alysson
Alta	Alyvia
Altagracia	Amaan
Altair	Amabel
Althaea	Amachi
Althea	Amadeus
Althia	Amado
Alton	Amador
Alun	Amaia
Alvaro	Amairani
Alvena	Amairany
Alvertos	Amal
Alvia	Amalia
Alvin	Aman

Amanda	Amelia
Amani	Amelie
Amapola	Amen
Amar	America
Amara	Americo
Amarah	Americus
Amaranth	Amerie
Amarantha	Amethyst
Amari	Ami
Amariah	Amia
Amarie	Amiah
Amarion	Amias
Amaris	Amida
Amaryllis	Amie
Amasa	Amilia
Amaterasu	Amin
Amaya	Amina
Amayah	Aminah
Ambar	Amir
Amber	Amira
Amberline	Amirah
Amberly	Amiya
Amboree	Amiyah
Ambretta	Ammar
Ambrose	Ammon
Ameer	Amor
Ameera	Amora

Amory
Amos
Amoura
Amphitrite
Amy
An
Ana
Anabel
Anabella
Anabelle
Anacletus
Anafa
Anahi
Anahit
Anahita
Anais
Anaisha
Anaiya
Anaiyah
Anakin
Analeah
Analee
Anali
Analia
Analiah
Analisa
Analise

Analiyah
Analy
Anant
Ananya
Anas
Anastasia
Anastasius
Anat
Anatase
Anatole
Anatolia
Anaya
Anayah
Anders
Anderson
Andi
Andie
Andraste
Andre
Andrea
Andreas
Andrei
Andres
Andrew
Androcles
Andromeda
Andy

Anemone	Anka
Anessa	Ann
Anezka	Ann/e
Angel	Anna
Angela	Annabel
Angelia	Annabell
Angelica	Annabella
Angelie	Annabelle
Angelina	Annabeth
Angeline	Annaisha
Angelique	Annaleah
Angelo	Annalee
Anghus	Annalia
Angie	Annalie
Angus	Annaliese
Ani	Annalisa
Ania	Annalise
Anika	Annamarie
Anisa	Annan
Anise	Anne
Anish	Annelise
Anisha	Annette
Anissa	Annie
Anita	Annika
Aniya	Annwfn
Aniyah	Annwn
Anjali	Anny

Annya	Anzu
Ansel	Aod
Anselm	Aodh
Ansgar	Aodhan
Ansh	Aoife
Ansley	Aonghus
Anson	Ap Owen
Anthea	Apastron
Anthony	Aphelion
Antigone	Aphria
Antipas	Aphrodite
Antoine	Apollo
Antoinette	Apollonia
Anton	Apostolos
Antonella	Apple
Antoni	April
Antonia	Aquila
Antonio	Aquilina
Antony	Ara
Antwan	Arabella
Anuhea	Arabelle
Anvi	Araceli
Anvika	Aracely
Anwell	Aragorn
Anwyl	Arakan
Anya	Araluen
Anyon	Aram

Araminta
Aramis
Aran
Arantxa
Arantza
Aranza
Arata
Arawn
Araya
Araylia
Arbor
Arcadia
Arcadio
Archer
Archibald
Archie
Ardell
Ardelle
Arden
Ardena
Ardene
Ardra
Arela
Areli
Arella
Arely
Ares

Aretha
Argyle
Arham
Ari
Aria
Ariadna
Ariadne
Ariah
Arian
Ariana
Arianna
Arianny
Ariany
Aribella
Aric
Arie
Ariel
Ariela
Ariella
Arielle
Arienh
Aries
Arild
Arina
Aris
Arisbeth
Arisu

Ariya	Armando
Ariyah	Armani
Arizbeth	Armstrong
Arjan	Arnas
Arjun	Arnav
Arkin	Arnold
Arlan	Arnost
Arlana	Aron
Arland	Arran
Arledge	Arron
Arleen	Arrow
Arleigh	Arroyo
Arlen	Art
Arlene	Artair
Arlet	Arte
Arleta	Artek
Arleth	Artemis
Arlett	Arthur
Arlette	Artie
Arley	Artis
Arlin	Arto
Arlina	Artur
Arline	Arturo
Arlo	Arty
Arlyn	Arun
Armaan	Arundel
Arman	Arvid

Arwen	Aston
Arya	Astrid
Aryan	Asuka
Aryana	Atarah
Aryanna	Athelstan
Asa	Athena
Asami	Atlantic
Asees	Atlas
Ash	Atreus
Asha	Atria
Ashanti	Atsushi
Ashby	Atticus
Asher	Attie
Ashley	Atty
Ashly	Atur
Ashlyn	Atziri
Ashlynn	Au
Ashton	Aubree
Ashwin	Aubrey
Asia	Aubri
Asiya	Aubriana
Asma	Aubrianna
Aspen	Aubrie
Asra	Aubriella
Assumpta	Aubrielle
Aster	Auburn
Asteria	Audelia

Auden
Audra
Audree
Audrey
Audriana
Audrianna
Audrie
Audrina
August
Augusta
Augustine
Augustus
Auk
Aulani
Aura
Aurelia
Aurelio
Aurelius
Aurora
Austen
Austin
Austin / Austen
Austyn
Autumn
Ava
Avah
Avalon

Avalyn
Avalynn
Avani
Aveline
Averi
Averie
Averill
Avery
Aviana
Avianna
Avigail
Avis
Aviva
Avleen
Avneet
Avni
Avocet
Avon
Avonlea
Avril
Avyanna
Awarnach
Awnan
Axel
Axl
Axton
Aya

Ayaan	Aza
Ayah	Azaan
Ayaka	Azalea
Ayako	Azami
Ayame	Azaria
Ayan	Azariah
Ayana	Azeneth
Ayanna	Aziel
Ayano	Azrael
Ayden	Azucena
Aydin	Azul
Ayesha	Azumi
Ayla	Azure
Aylani	
Ayleen	
Aylen	
Aylin	
Ayman	
Ayomide	
Ayoub	
Ayra	
Ayrton	
Ayub	
Ayumi	
Ayush	
Ayva	
Ayvah	

B

Baby
Baiji
Baikal
Bailee
Bailey
Baird
Bairrfhionn
Baker
Bali
Ballard
Balsam
Bancroft
Banks
Bannon
Banyan
Baptiste
Barbara
Barbary
Barclay
Bard
Barden
Bardon
Barkley

Barley
Barnaby
Barnett
Barney
Barra
Barracuda
Barrett
Barrie
Barry
Bartholomew
Bartlomiej
Bartosz
Basil
Bast
Baxter
Bay
Bayard
Baylee
Baylor
Bayo
Bayou
Bayre
Beacan
Beach
Beacher
Bean
Bear

Bearacb	Bellatrix
Bearcban	Belle
Beardsley	Bellerose
Beatha	Belva
Beatrice	Ben
Beatrix	Benas
Beatriz	Bendigeidfran
Beau	Benedict
Becan	Bénédicta
Beck	Benes
Beckett	Benicio
Beckham	Benita
Bede	Benito
Bedelia	Benjamin
Bedrich	Bennett
Bedwyr	Bennie
Beech	Benny
Begonia	Beno
Bela	Benoit
Belarius	Benson
Beldon	Bente
Belen	Bentlee
Belinda	Bentley
Bella	Berenice
Belladonna	Bergamot
Bellamy	Bergen
Bellarose	Berit

Berkeley	Bibiana
Berkley	Bijou
Berlin	Bilal
Bernadette	Bill
Bernard	Billie
Bernardo	Billy
Bernice	Billy/Billie
Berry	Bina
Berta	Birch
Bertie	Birdie
Beryl	Birgit
Bessie	Birk
Beta	Birkita
Betania	Birte
Betha	Bjarki
Bethany	Björk
Betony	Bjorn
Betsy	Blaine
Bettany	Blainey
Betty	Blair
Bevan	Blaire
Beverly	Blaise
Bevin	Blake
Bevyn	Blakeley
Bexley	Blakely
Bianca	Blanca
Bianka	Blanche

Blanchefleur
Blane
Blayke
Blayne
Blayney
Blaze
Blazej
Blessing
Blizzard
Blodwen
Bloom
Blossom
Blue
Bluebell
Blythe
Bo
Boaz
Bobbie
Bobby
Bobby / Bobbie
Bode
Boden
Bodhi
Bodie
Body
Bogdan
Bogdashka

Bohdan
Bohumil
Bohumir
Bohuslav
Bojan
Bojanek
Bojek
Bojik
Bolek
Boleslav
Bolide
Bonnie
Bonsai
Booker
Boone
Booth
Borden
Borivoj
Borys
Boston
Botan
Boulder
Bovra
Bovrek
Bovrik
Bovza
Bovzek

Bowden
Bowdyn
Bowen
Bowie
Bowyn
Boyd
Boyden
Boynton
Bozidar
Brad
Braden
Bradford
Bradley
Bradly
Brady
Braeden
Braelyn
Braelynn
Braiden
Bramble
Bran
Branch
Brandan
Branden
Brandon
Brangaine
Branik

Branislav
Brann
Branson
Brant
Brantley
Branwen
Brarn
Brasil
Bratislav
Braxton
Bray
Brayan
Brayden
Braydon
Braylee
Braylen
Braylon
Brazil
Brea
Breanainn
Breandan
Breanna
Breccia
Brecken
Bredon
Bree
Breeda

Breeze	Brian
Breezie	Briana
Breezy	Briann
Brencis	Brianna
Brenda	Briannah
Brendan	Brianne
Brenden	Briannon
Brendon	Briano
Brendt	Briant
Brenna	Briar
Brennan	Brice
Brennen	Bricriu
Brent	Brid
Brenten	Bride
Brentley	Bridger
Brently	Bridget
Brenton	Bridgette
Breslin	Bridie
Bressal	Briella
Bret	Brielle
Bretislav	Brien
Brett	Brienna
Bretta	Brienne
Brewster	Brietta
Bria	Briggs
Briac	Brigham
Briallen	Brighid

Brighton
Brigid
Brigitta
Brigitte
Brina
Brinicle
Brinley
Brion
Briony
Brisa
Briseida
Briseis
Briseyda
Brissa
Bristol
Brit
Brita
Brite
Brites
Britney
Britta
Brittany
Brittney
Brixton
Brock
Broderick
Brodie

Brody
Brogan
Broin
Bromley
Bronek
Bronislav
Bronislaw
Bronson
Bronwen
Bronwyn
Brook
Brooke
Brooklyn
Brooklynn
Brooks
Brown
Bruce
Brunhilda
Bruno
Bryan
Bryana
Bryann
Bryanna
Bryanne
Bryant
Bryce
Brycen

Bryden
Brygid
Brylee
Bryn
Brynlee
Brynn
Bryon
Bryony
Bryson
Bssil
Bubba
Buck
Buckley
Bud
Buddy
Budek
Budislav
Buffy
Bunko
Burdette
Burgess
Burke
Burl
Burle
Burne
Burt
Buster

Buttercup
Byron

C

Cabot
Cachamwri
Cadby
Cade
Cadell
Caden
Cadence
Cadman
Cady
Caedmon
Caelan
Caelum
Cagney
Cahal
Cai
Caia
Caiden
Cailyn
Caiman
Cain
Caio
Cairbre
Cairo

Caitlin
Caitlyn
Caius
Calantha
Calanthe
Calder
Caldera
Caldwell
Cale
Caleb
Caledonia
Calendula
Calhoun
Cali
Calia
Calista
Calix
Caliyah
Calla
Callahan
Callaia
Callan
Callen
Callie
Calliope
Callisto
Callum

Calum

Calvert

Calvin

Calypso

Calytrix

Cambria

Camden

Camdyn

Camellia

Cameo

Camero

Cameron

Camey

Camila

Camilla

Camille

Camilo

Camlin

Campbell

Campion

Camron

Camryn

Canaan

Candace

Candice

Candida

Candido

Candra

Candy

Canei

Canna

Cannon

Canon

Canton

Canute

Canyon

Caoilfhinnn

Caoimhe

Caoimhghin

Cappy

Capri

Car

Cara

Caradoc

Caraway

Carbry

Carden

Cardew

Carew

Carey

Carina

Carissa

Carl

Carla

Carleton

Carter

Carlie

Carter / Karter

Carlo

Caruso

Carlos

Carvell

Carlotta

Carwyn

Carlton

Cary

Carly

Cascade

Carlyle

Case

Carmel

Casen

Carmela

Casey

Carmella

Cash

Carmelo

Cason

Carmen

Caspar

Carmine

Casper

Carnation

Caspian

Carney

Cassandra

Carol

Cassava

Carole

Cassia

Carolina

Cassian

Caroline

Cassidy

Carolyn

Cassie

Carr

Cassiopeia

Carrie

Cassius

Carrington

Cassivellaunus

Carrol

Castiel

Carroll

Castor

Carson

Caswallan

Cataleya
Catalina
Catcher
Catena
Caterina
Cathair
Cathal
Cathaoir
Catherine
Cathleen
Cathy
Catkin
Cattaleya
Cattleya
Cave
Cayden
Caydence
Cayenne
Cayla
Caylee
Cayson
Cecelia
Cecil
Cecilia
Cecily
Cedar
Cedric

Celandine
Celeste
Celestia
Celestin
Celia
Celina
Celine
Celyddon
Celyn
Cerdwin
Cereus
Cerise
Cersei
Cesar
Ceslav
Chad
Chadwick
Chaim
Chan
Chana
Chance
Chandler
Chanel
Chanelle
Chaney
Channing
Chara

Charis
Charity
Charlee
Charleigh
Charlene
Charles
Charleston
Charley
Charli
Charlie
Charlie / Charley
Charlize
Charlotte
Chase
Chaya
Chaz
Che
Chelsea
Chelsey
Cheney
Cherish
Cherry
Chester
Chevelle
Chevy
Cheyenne
Chiara

Chiasa
Chieko
Chiharu
Chika
Chikako
Chilton
Chinami
Chitose
Chiyo
Chizu
Chloe
Chloé
Cho
Chris
Chris/Kris
Chrisoula
Christabel
Christian
Christiana
Christina
Christine
Christopher
Christy
Chrysalis
Cian
Ciara
Ciaran

Cici
Cielo
Cienna
Cierra
Cillian
Cindy
Cinnamon
Cinnia
Cinnie
Circe
Citlali
Citlalli
Citlaly
Citrine
Citron
Claiborne
Claire
Clancy
Clara
Clare
Clarence
Clarissa
Clark
Clarke
Claude
Claudia
Clay

Clayton
Clematis
Clemence
Clemensia
Clement
Clementine
Cleo
Cleome
Cleveland
Cliantha
Cliff
Clifford
Clifton
Clint
Clinton
Clive
Clodagh
Cloud
Clove
Clove/Clover
Clover
Clust
Clustfeinad
Clyde
Coalan
Cobalt
Coby

Cocidius

Coco

Codey

Codie

Cody

Cohen

Coinneach

Colbert

Colbie

Colborn

Colby

Cole

Coleman

Colette

Coleus

Colin

Colleen

Collette

Collin

Collins

Colm

Colombine

Colson

Colt

Coltan

Colten

Colter

Colton

Columba

Columbus

Comet

Con

Conal

Conall

Conall Cernach

Conan

Conant

Conchobar

Condan

Condon

Conn

Connal

Connell

Conner

Connie

Connla

Connor

Conor

Conrad

Conroy

Constance

Consuelo

Conway

Cooper

Copper

Cora

Coral

Coralie

Coraline

Corann

Corazon

Corban

Corben

Corbett

Corbin

Cordelia

Cordell

Corey

Corina

Corinna

Corinne

Corliss

Cormac

Cornel

Cornelia

Cornelius

Cortez

Cory

Corymbia

Cosette

Cosima

Cosimo

Cosmo

Cotton

Coty

Coulter

Courtenay

Courtland

Courtney

Cove

Coventina

Covey

Cowan

Cradawg

Crag

Craig

Crane

Crawford

Creed

Creek

Creighton

Creola

Crescent

Cressida

Crevasse

Crew

Cricket

Crisanta

Crispin
Cristal
Cristian
Cristina
Cristopher
Croix
Cromwell
Crosby
Cruz
Crystal
Ctibor
Ctik
Ctirad
Ctislav
Cuchulain
Cuinn
Culain
Culann
Cullen
Currier
Curtis
Custennin
Cuyler
Cyclone
Cygni
Cynthia
Cypress

Cyric
Cyril
Cyrilla
Cyrus

D

Dacey
Dacite
Daenerys
Daffodil
Dafne
Dahlia
Dai
Daichi
Dailyn
Daira
Daire
Daisuke
Daisy
Daitan
Dakari
Dakota
Dakota / Dakotah
Dal
Dalary
Dale
Dalek
Daleyza
Dalia

Daliah
Dalibor
Dalila
Dalilah
Dallas
Dalton
Daman
Damari
Damaris
Damek
Damian
Damien
Damion
Damon
Dan
Dana
Dana / Dane
Danae
Dandelion
Dandre
Dane
Danelly
Dangelo
Dangerfield
Dani
Dania
Danica

Daniel	Darla
Daniela	Darleen
Danielius	Darlene
Daniella	Darlyn
Danielle	Darnell
Danika	Darragh
Daniyal	Darrel
Danna	Darrel /Darryl /Daryl
Danner	Darrell
Danny	Darren
Dante	Darrick
Danu	Darrin
Danyal	Darrius
Daphne	Darryl
Daquan	Darsh
Dara	Daru
Darby	Darwin
Darcy	Darya
Daria	Daryl
Darian	Dash
Dariana	Dasha
Dariel	Dashawn
Darien	Dave
Darin	David
Dario	Davin
Darion	Davina
Darius	Davion

Davis	Defne
Davon	Deheune
Dawid	Deidre
Dawn	Deirdre
Dawood	Deja
Dawson	Delaney
Dawud	Delanie
Dax	Delano
Daxton	Delia
Dayana	Delilah
Dayanara	Della
Dayanna	Delmore
Dayra	Delphine
Dayton	Delta
Deacon	Delylah
Dean	Demarcus
Deandre	Demelza
Deangelo	Demetria
Deanna	Demetrius
Dearg	Demi
Debora	Dempsey
Deborah	Den
Dechtire	Denali
Declan	Denham
Dedric	Denis
Deen	Denise
Deepak	Denisse

Deniz
Dennis
Denver
Denzel
Denzil
Deoch
Deon
Deonte
Derecho
Derek
Derick
Dermot
Derowen
Derrick
Derry
Derya
Desdemona
Deshawn
Desiree
Desmond
Destin
Destinee
Destiny
Deutzia
Dev
Deva
Devan

Devante
Deven
Devin
Devina
Devnet
Devon
Devona
Devonte
Devyn
Dewain
Dewayne
Dewi
Dexter
Dhruv
Diamond
Diana
Diane
Dianella
Dianna
Diantha
Diego
Dierdre
Digby
Diggory
Dilan
Dilbert
Dillan

Dillion
Dillon
Dilys
Dimitri
Dimona
Dina
Dinah
Dinsmore
Dion
Dione
Dior
Dirk
Dita
Diva
Divakar
Divine
Divone
Dixie
Diya
Dobromil
Dobromir
Dobroslav
Doirean
Dolores
Domhnall
Dominic
Dominick

Dominik
Dominique
Dominykas
Don
Donaghy
Donal
Donald
Donall
Donat
Donatella
Donati
Donavan
Donella
Donia
Donna
Donnally
Donnchadh
Donnell
Donnelly
Donnie
Donogb
Donovan
Donte
Dora
Doran
Doreen
Doreena

Dorian	Driskell
Doris	Druce
Dorothea	Drudwyn
Dorothy	Drummond
Dorran	Duane
Dorset	Duby
Dory	Dudley
Dosne	Duer
Doug	Duff
Dougal	Duffey
Doughal	Duffy
Doughlas	Dughall
Dougie	Duke
Douglas	Dulce
Dove	Dumin
Dover	Duncan
Doy	Dune
Doyle	Dunham
Draco	Dunja
Drake	Dunley
Dream	Dunn
Dree	Duran
Drem	Durko
Drever	Durward
Drew	Dusa
Driscol	Dusan
Driscoll	Dusanek

Dustin
Dusty
Duysek
Dwayne
Dwight
Dyfed
Dylan

E

Ea
Eagan
Eagle
Eamon
Earhart
Earl
Earnest
Eartha
Easterly
Easton
Eastyn
Ebba
Eben
Ebony
Eburscon
Echidna
Eda
Edan
Edana
Edda
Eddie
Eddy
Edelweiss

Eden
Edgar
Edie
Edison
Edith
Edmund
Edna
Edrei
Edsel
Eduardo
Edward
Edwin
Eesa
Efnisien
Efrain
Egan
Egeria
Egerton
Eghan
Eglantine
Egypt
Ehsan
Eibhlín
Eichi
Eike
Eiko
Eila

Eileen

Eilon

Eimy

Einion

Eira

Eirene

Eisa

Eisley

Eithan

Eiza

Ekaterina

Ela

Eladio

Elaina

Elaine

Elam

Elan

Elara

Elayna

Elder

Eldon

Eldora

Eldoris

Eldred

Eldridge

Eleanor

Eleanora

Elena

Eleni

Elestren

Elettra

Elfrida

Elgin

Elgine

Eli

Elia

Elian

Eliana

Elianna

Elias

Elidor

Eliel

Eliette

Elif

Elijah

Elin

Elina

Elinor

Eliot

Elis

Elisa

Elisabeth

Elise

Eliseo

Elisha	Elmore
Eliska	Elodea
Elissa	Elodie
Eliyanah	Eloisa
Eliza	Eloise
Elizabella	Elon
Elizabeth	Elora
Elizah	Elowen
Eljin	Elroy
Ella	Elsa
Elle	Elsha
Ellen	Elsie
Ellery	Elton
Ellia	Elva
Elliana	Elvina
Ellianna	Elvira
Ellie	Elvis
Elliot	Elwood
Elliot / Elliott	Elyana
Elliott	Elyse
Ellis	Elysia
Ellison	Elyssa
Elly	Ema
Elm	Emani
Elmer	Emanuel
Elmira	Emanuele
Elmo	Emarie

Embelia

Ember

Emberly

Emelia

Emelie

Emeline

Emely

Emerald

Emeri

Emerie

Emerson

Emersyn

Emery

Emery / Emory

Emi

Emiko

Emil

Emile

Emilee

Emilia

Emiliana

Emiliano

Emilie

Emilio

Emily

Emir

Emiyo

Emlyn

Emma

Emmalee

Emmaline

Emmalyn

Emmalynn

Emmanuel

Emmanuelle

Emmarie

Emmarose

Emme

Emmeline

Emmet

Emmett

Emmi

Emmie

Emmitt

Emmy

Emory

Emre

Emrie

Emry

Emrys

Ena

Eneco

Engl

Enid

Enoch
Enola
Enrico
Enrique
Ensley
Enya
Enzo
Eoghan
Eoghann
Eoin
Eos
Eowyn
Ephraim
Ephron
Equinox
Eranthe
Erasmo
Erea
Eren
Eri
Eric
Erica
Erich
Erick
Ericka
Erie
Erik

Erika
Erin
Erina
Eris
Erity
Erlina
Erlinda
Erma
Ermias
Ermine
Erna
Ernest
Ernestine
Ernesto
Ernie
Errol
Erskine
Ervin
Erwin
Eryk
Eryn
Esa
Escallonia
Eshaan
Eshan
Esme
Esmeralda

Esmond
Esperanza
Esteban
Estefania
Estefany
Estela
Estella
Estelle
Ester
Estevan
Esther
Estrella
Estuary
Etain
Etana
Eternity
Ethan
Ethel
Ethne
Etienne
Etsu
Etsuko
Etta
Euan
Eudora
Eugene
Eugenia

Eugenie
Euglena
Eulalia
Eunice
Euphemia
Eva
Evadne
Evalina
Evalyn
Evalynn
Evan
Evangelina
Evangeline
Evanthe
Eve
Evelin
Evelina
Eveline
Evelyn
Evelynn
Ever
Everard
Everest
Everett
Evergreen
Everlee
Everleigh

Everley
Everly
Evette
Evi
Evie
Evolet
Evonne
Evora
Evza
Evzek
Evzen
Evzenek
Ewald
Ewan
Ewen
Ewyn
Exton
Ezekiel
Ezequiel
Ezra
Ezume

F

Faber
Fabia
Fabian
Fabienne
Fabiola
Fahad
Fainche
Fairfax
Faisal
Faith
Faizaan
Faizan
Falcon
Fallon
Fanousek
Farah
Fardoragh
Farhan
Farica
Faris
Farley
Faron
Farrah

Farran
Farrel
Farrell
Farren
Farrin
Fatima
Fauna
Faustino
Fawn
Faye
Fayola
Fearghus
Feather
Fedelm
Feichin
Felan
Felicia
Felicity
Felipe
Felix
Fen
Fenella
Fennel
Fenton
Ferdinand
Ferehar
Ferghus

Fergus
Ferguson
Fern
Fernanda
Fernando
Ferrell
Ferris
Ffion
Fflur
Fiachra
Fiacra
Fiacre
Fianna
Fidel
Field
Fielding
Fifi
Fig
Figueroa
Filber
Filip
Finbar
Finch
Findabair
Findlay
Fineas
Fineen

Finghin
Fingula
Finian
Finlay
Finley
Finn
Finnbar
Finneen
Finnegan
Finnian
Finnin
Finnlay
Finnley
Finnobarr
Finola
Fintan
Fiona
Fionan
Fionn
Fionnbarr
Fiora
Fioralba
Fiorella
Fiorello
Firth
Fisher
Fitzgerald

Fiynn	Floyd
Fjord	Flyn
Flainn	Flynn
Flanagan	Fogartaigh
Flann	Fogarty
Flanna	Fogerty
Flannagain	Foley
Flannagan	Forbes
Flannan	Ford
Flannery	Forest
Fletcher	Forrest
Fleur	Forsythia
Flinn	Fossa
Flint	Fossil
Floinn	Foster
Floortje	Fox
Flor	Foxglove
Flora	Frana
Florence	Frances
Florent	Francesca
Florentina	Francesco
Florian	Francine
Florida	Francis
Florin	Francis / Frances
Florine	Francisco
Florizel	Franciszek
Flower	Franco

Franek

Frank

Frankie

Franklin

Franky

Franta

Frantik

Frantisek

Fraser

Frazer

Fred

Freddie

Freddy

Frederic

Frederick

Fredrick

Freedom

Freesia

Freya

Freyja

Frida

Frost

Fuchsia

Fudo

Fujita

Fuller

Fulton

Fumiko

Furman

Fynbar

Fynn

G

Gabriel
Gabriela
Gabriella
Gabrielle
Gadhra
Gael
Gaffney
Gage
Gaia
Gaile
Gaines
Gair
Gala
Galanthus
Galatea
Galaxy
Gale
Galena
Gali
Galilea
Galileah
Galileo
Gall

Gallagher
Galvin
Galvyn
Gannon
Gar
Garance
Gardenia
Gardner
Gareth
Garfield
Garland
Garnet
Garret
Garrett
Garrison
Garry
Gary
Gatlin
Gavin
Gawain
Gelso
Gem
Gema
Gemini
Gemma
Gen
Gene

Gene / Jean	Gia
Genesis	Giacinta
Geneva	Giacomo
Genevie	Giada
Genevieve	Giana
Genki	Giancarlo
Gentry	Gianina
Geoffrey	Gianna
George	Gianni
Georgia	Giavanna
Georgie	Gideon
Georgina	Gigi
Gerald	Gilbert
Geraldine	Gilberto
Geranium	Gilda
Gerard	Gildas
Gerardo	Gilford
Germaine	Gilia
German	Gillian / Jillian
Geronimo	Gilmore
Gert	Gilroy
Gertie	Gin
Gertrude	Gina
Gervase	Ginebra
Gesa	Ginerva
Gethin	Ginessa
Gharial	Ginger

Ginkgo
Gino
Gio
Giovanna
Giovanni
Gisela
Gisele
Giselle
Gisselle
Gitta
Giulia
Giuliana
Giulianna
Giulietta
Gizelle
Glacier
Gladiola
Gladys
Glen
Glen / Glenn
Glenn
Glenna
Glifieu
Gloria
Glory
Glyn
Glynis

Godiva
Golda
Golden
Goldie
Goldman
Gonzalo
Gordon
Goro
Gorsedd
Gower
Grace
Gracelyn
Gracelynn
Gracie
Graciela
Grady
Graham
Gráinne
Grania
Granite
Grant
Granville
Gratia
Gray
Gray / Grey
Graydon
Graysen

Grayson	Gulliver
Grazia	Gunnar
Grecia	Gunner
Green	Gunther
Greer	Gurnoor
Greg	Gus
Gregg	Gustave
Gregory	Gustavo
Greta	Guy
Gretchen	Gwalchmai
Grettel	Gwawl
Grey	Gwen
Greyson	Gwendolen
Griffin	Gwendolin
Griselda	Gwendolyn
Grove	Gweneth
Grover	Gwenith
Groves	Gwenn
Gruddieu	Gwenneth
Guadalupe	Gwenyth
Gudrun	Gwenyver
Guenevere	Gwern
Guennola	Gwernaeh
Guillermo	Gwri
Guinevere	Gwydion
Gulf	Gwyndolin
Gull	Gwyneth

Gwynham
Gwynith
Gwynn

H

Haaris
Hachiro
Hadar
Hadassah
Hadden
Hadi
Hadlee
Hadleigh
Hadley
Hadwin
Hagley
Haiden
Haider
Hail
Hailee
Hailey
Hailie
Haisley
Hajime
Hake
Halbert
Halcyon
Haley

Hali
Hall
Hallam
Halle
Halley
Hallie
Halo
Halsey
Hamal
Hamilton
Hamish
Hampton
Hamza
Hamzah
Hana
Hanako
Hanan
Haneen
Haniya
Hank
Hanna
Hannah
Hannibal
Hans
Hapuka
Harbor
Hardy

Hari	Haruki
Haris	Harun
Harlan	Haruo
Harland	Harvey
Harlee	Hasan
Harleen	Haseeb
Harleigh	Hashim
Harlem	Haskell
Harley	Hasnain
Harlie	Hassan
Harlow	Hastings
Harlowe	Hattie
Harlyn	Havana
Harman	Havelock
Harmon	Haven
Harmoni	Hawa
Harmony	Hawk
Harold	Hawthorn
Haroon	Hawthorne
Harper	Haya
Harri	Hayami
Harriet	Hayden
Harris	Haydn
Harrison	Hayes
Harry	Haylee
Hart	Hayley
Haru	Haylie

Haywood	Henrik
Hazel	Henry
Hazelton	Henwas
Heath	Herb
Heather	Herbert
Heaven	Herbie
Heavenly	Hercules
Hector	Heriberto
Hedley	Herman
Hedwig	Hermione
Hefeydd	Herne
Heidi	Hero
Heidy	Hertha
Heilyn	Hester
Helen	Heywood
Helena	Hezekiah
Heliodor	Hide
Heliotrope	Hideki
Hellen	Hideko
Hemlock	Hideo
Henbeddestr	Hideyo
Hendrick	Hikaru
Hendrix	Hilario
Henley	Hilda
Henna	Hildegarde
Hennessy	Hill
Henri	Hilliard

Hilton	Horton
Hirkani	Hosanna
Hiro	Hoshi
Hiroki	Hotaru
Hirola	Houston
Hiromi	Howard
Hiroshi	Howl
Hiroyuki	Hoyt
Hisa	Huarwar
Hisano	Hubbell
Hisoka	Hubert
Hobart	Huckleberry
Hodge	Hudson
Hoki	Hueil
Holden	Huey
Hollace	Hugh
Holland	Hugo
Hollis	Hulda
Holly	Hulk
Holmes	Humbert
Homer	Humberto
Honesty	Humphrey
Honey	Humza
Honor	Hunt
Honorius	Hunter
Hope	Huon
Horace	Hurley

Husna
Hussain
Hussein
Hutton
Huw
Huxley
Hyacinth
Hyatt
Hydnora
Hydra
Hydrangea
Hydrilla
Hyrum

I

Iago
Ian
Ianthe
Ianto
Ibex
Ibraheem
Ibrahim
Ichabod
Ichigo
Ida
Idelisa
Idelle
Iden
Idina
Ido
Idra
Idris
Iestyn
Ieuan
Ifan
Ignacio
Igor
Ihsan

Ike
Iker
Iku
Ila
Ilan
Ilana
Ilara
Ileana
Ilene
Iliana
Illiana
Ilona
Iluka
Ilyas
Iman
Imani
Imogen
Imran
Inaaya
Inanna
Inara
Inaya
Inayah
Indi
India
Indiana
Indie

Indigo	Isa
Indri	Isaac
Ine	Isabel
Ines	Isabela
Inez	Isabell
Ingrid	Isabella
Inigo	Isabelle
Inness	Isadora
Innis	Isaiah
Io	Isaias
Ioan	Isao
Iolanthe	Isela
Iona	Isha
Ione	Ishaan
Ira	Ishaq
Ireland	Ishika
Irelynn	Isiah
Irene	Isla
Irie	Isle
Iris	Ismaeel
Irit	Ismael
Irlanda	Ismail
Irma	Isobel
Irven	Isold
Irvin	Isolda
Irving	Isolde
Irvyn	Israel

Issa
Issac
Italia
Italy
Ito
Itzamara
Itzayana
Itzel
Itzia
Iva
Ivan
Ivana
Ivanka
Ivanna
Ivara
Ives
Ivette
Ivo
Ivor
Ivory
Ivy
Iwan
Ixia
Ixora
Iyla
Izaac
Izaak

Izaan
Izabel
Izabella
Izabelle
Izaiah
Izanagi
Izara
Izel

J

Jabari
Jac
Jacaranda
Jace
Jacey
Jacinda
Jacinta
Jack
Jackeline
Jackie
Jackie / Jaqui
Jacklyn
Jacklynn
Jackson
Jaclyn
Jacob
Jacoby
Jacqueline
Jacquelyn
Jad
Jada
Jade
Jaden

Jaden /Jayden / Jaidyn
Jadiel
Jadon
Jaeden
Jael
Jaelyn
Jaelynn
Jagger
Jago
Jaguar
Jai
Jaida
Jaiden
Jailyne
Jaime
Jair
Jairo
Jak
Jakari
Jake
Jakob
Jakub
Jalen
Jaliyah
Jamaal
Jamaica
Jamal

Jamar	Janney
Jamari	Janus
Jamel	Japheth
James	Jaquan
James / Jamie / Jayme	Jaqueline
Jameson	Jared
Jamie	Jaretzy
Jamil	Jarita
Jamila	Jarlath
Jamileth	Jarod
Jamir	Jarom
Jamison	Jaron
Jan	Jarrah
Jana	Jarred
Janae	Jarrell
Jane	Jarrett
Janella	Jarrod
Janelle	Jarvis
Janelly	Jase
Janessa	Jasiah
Janet	Jasleen
Janeth	Jaslene
Janice	Jaslyn
Janie	Jasmin
Janine	Jasmine
Janiyah	Jason
Janna	Jasper

Javier

Javion

Javon

Javor

Jax

Jaxen

Jaxon

Jaxson

Jaxton

Jaxx

Jaxxon

Jay

Jayce

Jaycee

Jayceon

Jaycie

Jayda

Jaydan

Jayde

Jayden

Jayden-lee

Jaydon

Jayla

Jaylah

Jaylani

Jaylee

Jayleen

Jaylen

Jaylene

Jaylie

Jaylin

Jayline

Jaylon

Jaylyn

Jaylynn

Jayne

Jayson

Jazelle

Jaziah

Jaziel

Jazleen

Jazlene

Jazlyn

Jazlynn

Jazmin

Jazmine

Jazmyn

Jazzlyn

Jean

Jeanette

Jedidiah

Jeevan

Jeff

Jefferson

Jeffery

Jeffrey

Jelena

Jemima

Jemma

Jenelle

Jenesis

Jenevieve

Jenna

Jennie

Jennifer

Jenny

Jennyfer

Jennyver

Jensen

Jenson

Jerald

Jeremiah

Jeremias

Jeremy

Jeriah

Jericho

Jermaine

Jerome

Jerrod

Jerry

Jeryl

Jesiah

Jeslyn

Jess

Jessa

Jessamine

Jessamy

Jesse

Jesse / Jessie

Jessi

Jessica

Jessie

Jesslyn

Jesus

Jet

Jethetha

Jethro

Jett

Jewel

Jhene

Jia

Jianna

Jillian

Jim

Jimena

Jimmie

Jimmy

Jin

Jiro
Jiselle
Jiya
Joan
Joana
Joanna
Joanne
Joaquin
Joben
Jocelyn
Jocelyne
Jocelynn
Jody
Joe
Joel
Joelle
Joesph
Joey
Johan
Johana
Johanna
Johannes
John
John-james
Johnathan
Johnathon
Johnnie

Johnny
Joie
Jolee
Jolene
Jolie
Jon
Jonah
Jonas
Jonathan
Jonathon
Jonny
Jonquil
Jonty
Jordan
Jordon
Jordy
Jordyn
Jordynn
Jorge
Jose
Josef
Josefina
Joselin
Joselyn
Joseph
Josephina
Josephine

Josh	Julia
Joshua	Julian
Josiah	Juliana
Josie	Juliane
Joslyn	Julianna
Josselyn	Julianne
Josslyn	Julie
Josue	Julien
Journee	Juliet
Journey	Julieta
Journi	Julieth
Jovan	Julietta
Jovanni	Juliette
Jovie	Julio
Joy	Julissa
Joyce	Julius
Joziah	Jun
Juan	Juna
Juanita	Junaid
Jubilee	June
Judah	Junior
Jude	Juniper
Judith	Junko
Judson	Juno
Judy	Jupiter
Juelz	Jurnee
Jules	Justice

Justin
Justine
Justus

K

Kabir
Kace
Kacey
Kacper
Kade
Kaden
Kadence
Kadin
Kaede
Kaeden
Kaelan
Kaelani
Kaelyn
Kaelynn
Kai
Kaia
Kaidan
Kaiden
Kaidence
Kaie
Kaila
Kailah
Kailani

Kailee
Kailey
Kaily
Kailyn
Kaimana
Kaine
Kaira
Kairi
Kairo
Kaiser
Kaisley
Kaison
Kaitlyn
Kaitlynn
Kaiya
Kaiyo
Kajus
Kalani
Kale
Kalea
Kaleah
Kaleb
Kalel
Kalena
Kaley
Kali
Kalia

Kaliah
Kalila
Kalina
Kaliyah
Kallie
Kallum
Kamal
Kamari
Kamden
Kamdyn
Kameko
Kameron
Kamil
Kamila
Kamilah
Kamilla
Kamille
Kamiyah
Kamran
Kamryn
Kamryn / Camryn
Kana
Kanaye
Kane
Kannon
Kano
Kantuta

Kaori
Kara
Karam
Kareem
Karely
Karen
Kari
Karim
Karina
Karis
Karisma
Karissa
Karl
Karla
Karlee
Karleen
Karley
Karlie
Karma
Karney
Karol
Karolina
Karoline
Karri
Karson
Karsyn
Karter

Kase	Katrina
Kasen	Katsumi
Kasey	Katy
Kash	Katya
Kashton	Kauri
Kason	Kavya
Kasper	Kawa
Kassandra	Kay
Kassia	Kaya
Kassiani	Kayan
Kassidy	Kaycee
Kataleya	Kayden
Katalina	Kaydence
Katarina	Kaydon
Katashi	Kayla
Kate	Kaylah
Katelyn	Kaylan
Katelynn	Kaylani
Katerina	Kaylee
Katharine	Kayleen
Katherine	Kayleigh
Kathleen	Kaylen
Kathryn	Kaylene
Kathy	Kayley
Katia	Kayli
Katie	Kaylie
Katja	Kaylin

Kaylum	Keir
Kaylynn	Keira
Kayne	Keiran
Kaysen	Keiron
Kayson	Keiry
Kazashi	Keith
Keagan	Keith / Keath
Keaghan	Kelby
Keane	Kellan
Keanu	Kellen
Kearney	Kelly
Keary	Kelp
Keaton	Kelsea
Keegan	Kelsey
Keelan	Kelsie
Keeley	Kelton
Keelia	Kelvan
Keelin	Kelven
Keely	Kelvin
Keenan	Kelvyn
Keene	Kelwin
Kegan	Kelwyn
Kehlani	Kemp
Kei	Ken
Keila	Kendal
Keilani	Kendall
Keily	Kendhal

Kendon
Kendra
Kendrick
Kenelm
Kenia
Kenley
Kenna
Kennedi
Kennedy
Kennedy / Kennedi
Kenneth
Kennocha
Kenny
Kensington
Kensley
Kent
Kentigem
Kentigern
Kenton
Kenya
Kenyon
Kenzie
Kenzo
Keon
Keren
Kermit
Kermode

Kerrigan
Kerry
Kerwin
Kerwyn
Keturah
Kevan
Keven
Kevin
Kevyn
Keyaan
Keyla
Keyon
Kezia
Keziah
Khadija
Khaleesi
Khalia
Khalid
Khalil
Khari
Khloe
Kiaan
Kian
Kiana
Kianna
Kiara
Kiera

Kieran	Kirra
Kieron	Kirrily
Kiley	Kirsten
Kilian	Kirwin
Killian	Kirwyn
Kim	Kit
Kim / Kym	Kitty
Kimana	Kizzy
Kimani	Klarissa
Kimber	Knightley
Kimberley	Knoll
Kimberly	Knox
Kimora	Koa
King	Kobe
Kingsley	Kobi
Kingston	Kobie
Kinley	Koby
Kinsey	Koda
Kinslee	Kodi
Kinsley	Kody
Kinzley	Kofi
Kipling	Kohana
Kipp	Kohen
Kira	Kojo
Kiran	Kolby
Kiri	Kole
Kirk	Kolten

Kolton	Krystian
Komal	Krzysztof
Konrad	Kuba
Konstantina	Kudu
Kop	Kunsgnos
Kora	Kurt
Korbin	Kurtis
Korey	Kya
Kori	Kyan
Korra	Kyara
Kory	Kye
Kosmo	Kyla
Krew	Kylah
Krill	Kylan
Kris	Kylar
Krish	Kyle
Krisha	Kylee
Kristen	Kyleigh
Kristian	Kylen
Kristin	Kyler
Kristina	Kylian
Kristine	Kylie
Kristofer	Kylin
Kristopher	Kyllion
Kristy	Kylo
Kruze	Kyng
Krystal	Kynlee

Kynthelig
Kyoko
Kyra
Kyran
Kyree
Kyrie
Kyro
Kyron
Kyros
Kyson

L

Laban
Lacey
Lachlan
Lacy
Ladd
Ladislav
Lady
Lagoon
Laguna
Laila
Lailah
Lailani
Lainey
Lairgnen
Laith
Lake
Lamar
Lamont
Lamprey
Lana
Lance
Land
Landen

Landon
Landry
Landyn
Lane
Laney
Lang
Langston
Lani
Laniyah
Lapis
Lapu
Lara
Laramie
Lareina
Larimar
Larissa
Lark
Larkspur
Larry
Latimer
Laura
Lauraine
Laurel
Lauren
Laurence
Laurence / Lawrence
Laurie

Lauryn	Leela
Lava	Leen
Lavena	Leena
Lavender	Legacy
Lavinia	Legend
Lawrence	Legolas
Lawson	Leia
Laya	Leigh
Layah	Leighton
Layan	Leila
Layla	Leilah
Laylah	Leilani
Laylani	Leilanie
Layne	Leilany
Layton	Leith
Lazarus	Lela
Lea	Leland
Leaf	Lemon
Leah	Lena
Leander	Leni
Leandro	Lenna
Leanna	Lennie
Leanne	Lennon
Leda	Lennox
Ledger	Lenny
Lee	Lenore
Lee / Leigh	Leo

Leon
Leona
Leonard
Leonardo
Leonel
Leonidas
Leonie
Leonora
Leopold
Leroy
Lesley
Leslie
Leslie / Lesley
Lesly
Lester
Leticia
Letitia
Levi
Levon
Lewie
Lewis
Lexa
Lexi
Lexie
Leyla
Leylah
Leylani

Leyton
Lia
Liah
Liam
Lian
Liana
Lianna
Libby
Liberty
Libra
Lidia
Liko
Lila
Lilac
Lilah
Lili
Lilia
Lilian
Liliana
Liliane
Lilianna
Lilias
Liliosa
Lilit
Lilith
Lilium
Lillian

Lilliana	Lisette
Lillianna	Lita
Lillie	Litton
Lillith	Litzy
Lilly	Liu
Lillyana	Liv
Lillyanna	Livia
Lilou	Liya
Lily	Liyana
Lilyana	Liz
Lilyanna	Liza
Lina	Lizar
Lincoln	Lizbeth
Lind	Lizeth
Linda	Lizette
Linden	Llewellyn
Lindsay	Llewelyn
Lindsey	Lloyd
Linette	Lluvia
Ling	Llyr
Linnea	Loch
Linnette	Lochlan
Linus	Locke
Lionel	Logan
Liora	Lois
Lir	Loki
Lisa	Lola

London	Lowri
Londyn	Loyalty
Ione	Luana
Lonnie	Luba
Lorcan	Luc
Lorelai	Luca
Lorelei	Lucas
Loren	Lucca
Lorena	Lucero
Lorenzo	Lucia
Loretta	Lucian
Lori	Lucian / Lucy-Ann
Lorna	Luciana
Lorne	Lucianna
Lorraine	Luciano
Lottie	Lucie
Lotus	Lucien
Lou	Lucienne
Loui	Lucille
Louie	Lucinda
Louis	Lucius
Louisa	Lucy
Louise	Ludmilla
Lourdes	Luella
Love	Luis
Lovely	Luisa
Lowell	Luka

Lukas

Lyre

Lukasz

Lyric

Luke

Lula

Lulu

Lumi

Luna

Lupin

Lupita

Luqman

Luther

Lux

Luxovious

Luz

Lyanna

Lydia

Lyla

Lylah

Lyle

Lyman

Lyndon

Lynet

Lynette

Lynn

Lynx

Lyonesse

Lyra

M

Mab
Mabel
Mabina
Mabon
Mac
Macauley
Maccus
Mace
Macey
Macey/Macy
Maci
Macie
Maciej
Mack
Mackenzie
Macklin
Macklyn
Macon
Macsen
Macy
Mada
Madaio
Madalyn

Madalynn
Madden
Maddie
Maddison
Maddock
Maddox
Madeiran
Madeleine
Madelief
Madeline
Madelyn
Madelyne
Madelynn
Madilyn
Madilynn
Madison
Madisyn
Madyson
Mae
Maeve
Maeveen
Magali
Magaly
Magdalena
Magdalene
Maggie
Magnolia

Magnus

Maha

Mahdi

Mahir

Mahogany

Mahoney

Mai

Maia

Maida

Mailen

Maine

Maira

Maisie

Maison

Maite

Maitland

Maiya

Maize

Majesty

Major

Makai

Makayla

Makena

Makenna

Makenzie

Makepeace

Maksim

Maksymilian

Malachi

Malachy

Malak

Malakai

Malakhi

Malani

Malaya

Malayah

Malaysia

Malcolm

Maleah

Malena

Mali

Malia

Maliah

Malik

Malina

Maliya

Maliyah

Mallory

Malus

Malvin

Malvina

Malvyn

Mamie

Mandrake

Mandy
Maneh
Manfred
Manley
Mannat
Manning
Mannix
Manraj
Mansi
Manuel
Manuka
Manzi
Maple
Mar
Mara
Marbella
Marble
Marc
Marcel
Marcela
Marceline
Marcella
Marcello
Marcellus
Marcelo
Marco
Marcos

Marcus
Marden
Marek
Marella
Marely
Maren
Margaret
Margarita
Margaux
Margo
Margot
Marguerite
Mari
Maria
Mariah
Mariam
Marian
Mariana
Marianna
Marianne
Maribel
Maribelle
Maricela
Marie
Mariel
Mariela
Mariella

Marielle	Marlin
Marigold	Marlo
Marilla	Marlon
Marilyn	Marlow
Marina	Marlowe
Marine	Marmaduke
Mariner	Marques
Marino	Marquis
Mario	Marquise
Marion	Mars
Maris	Marsden
Marisa	Marsh
Marisol	Marshall
Marissa	Martha
Maritza	Martin
Mariyah	Marty
Marjeta	Marvin
Marjoram	Marvina
Marjorie	Marvyn
Mark	Marwa
Markus	Mary
Marla	Maryam
Marlee	Maryjane
Marleigh	Mason
Marlene	Massif
Marley	Matas
Marlie	Mateo

Mateusz	Maximillian
Mather	Maximo
Mathew	Maximus
Mathias	Maxine
Matias	Maxton
Matilda	Maxwell
Matt	May
Matteo	Maya
Matthew	Mayah
Matthias	Mayeli
Mattie	Mayleen
Maude	Maylin
Maura	Maynard
Maureen	Mayo
Maurice	Mayra
Mauricio	Mayson
Mavelle	Mayte
Maven	Mazie
Maverick	Mazzy
Mavie	Mckayla
Mavis	Mckenna
Mawar	Mckenzie
Max	Mckinley
Maxi	Md
Maxim	Mead
Maximilian	Meadghbh
Maximiliano	Meadow

Meadowlark

Medb

Medredydd

Meera

Megan

Meghan

Mehar

Mehmet

Mei

Meilani

Mekhi

Mekong

Melani

Melania

Melanie

Melannie

Melany

Melia

Melina

Melinda

Melisa

Melisende

Melissa

Melodie

Melody

Melva

Melville

Melvin

Melvina

Melvyn

Memphis

Menw

Mercedes

Mercer

Mercury

Mercy

Mere

Meredith

Merida

Meriel

Merit

Meriwether

Merlin

Merlyn

Merna

Merrick

Merrigan

Merrill

Merritt

Merry

Mert

Merton

Mervin

Meryl

Mesa
Messiah
Metztli
Mia
Miabella
Miah
Mica
Micaela
Micah
Michael
Michaela
Michal
Micheal
Michelangelo
Michelle
Michon
Michonne
Mickey
Micky
Migdalia
Mignon
Miguel
Mika
Mikaeel
Mikaela
Mikail
Mikayla

Mike
Mikel
Mikey
Mikhail
Mikolaj
Mila
Milagro
Milagros
Milah
Milan
Milana
Milani
Milania
Mileena
Milena
Miles
Miley
Miliana
Milla
Millaray
Millard
Miller
Millicent
Millie
Milly
Milo
Milosz

Milton	Moana
Mimosa	Modesto
Mina	Mohamad
Minerva	Mohamed
Minka	Mohammad
Minnie	Mohammed
Mira	Mohsin
Mirabella	Moina
Mirabelle	Moira
Miracle	Moises
Mirage	Mollie
Miranda	Molly
Mireya	Mona
Miriam	Monica
Mirna	Monique
Miro	Monroe
Mirta	Monserrat
Mirth	Monserrate
Misael	Monserrath
Misha	Montague
Missy	Montana
Mist	Monte
Misty	Montgomery
Mitchel	Montserrat
Mitchell	Monty
Miya	Moon
Miyah	Mor

Mordechai
Moreen
Morfran
Morgan
Morgana
Morgance
Morgandy
Morgane
Moriah
Morna
Morrigan
Morris
Morrisey
Morton
Morven
Morvyn
Morwenna
Moryn
Moses
Moshe
Moss
Moya
Moyna
Muguet
Muhammad
Muhammed
Mujtaba

Mulberry
Mull
Mungo
Murdoc
Murdoch
Murdock
Muriel
Murphy
Murray
Murry
Murtagh
Musa
Musab
Mustafa
Mya
Myah
Myla
Mylah
Mylene
Myles
Mylo
Mynogan
Myra
Myrna
Myron
Myrthe
Myrtle

N

Nabil
Nadia
Nadine
Nahla
Nahomi
Nahomy
Naia
Naiad
Naila
Nailah
Naim
Naima
Nairn
Nala
Nalani
Naliyah
Nana
Nanala
Nancy
Nanette
Naois
Naomi
Naomy

Naphtali
Napoleon
Nara
Narcissa
Nardos
Nareen
Nareena
Nareene
Nash
Nasir
Nasrin
Natalee
Natalia
Natalie
Nataly
Natalya
Natan
Nataniel
Nataniele
Natasha
Nate
Nathalia
Nathalie
Nathaly
Nathan
Nathanael
Nathanial

Nathaniel	Nelda
Natron	Nell
Nature	Nellie
Nautilus	Nelly
Naveah	Nels
Navy	Nelson
Navya	Nemausus
Naya	Nemertea
Nayeli	Nemi
Nayla	Nemo
Nazayia	Neo
Neal	Nephi
Neala	Neptune
Neale	Neri
Nealie	Nerida
Nealon	Nerissa
Nebula	Nesto
Ned	Nestor
Nedes	Nettie
Neeja	Neva
Neema	Nevada
Neese	Nevaeh
Nefertari	Neveah
Nehemiah	Neville
Neil	Newell
Neill	Newland
Neilson	Newlin

Newlyn
Newman
Ngaio
Nia
Niall
Niallan
Niamh
Nicholas
Nichole
Nick
Nickolas
Nicky
Nico
Nicolas
Nicole
Nicolette
Niece
Nigel
Nigella
Nihal
Nika
Nike
Nikhil
Nikita
Nikki
Niklaus
Niko

Nikodem
Nikolai
Nikolas
Nila
Nile
Nima
Nimbus
Nimrod
Nina
Nirvana
Nisien
Nita
Nitella
Nixie
Nixon
Niya
Niyah
Noa
Noah
Noe
Noel
Noel / Noelle
Noelani
Noelia
Noelle
Noemi
Nohemi

Nojus

Nola

Nolan

Noland

Nona

Noor

Noora

Nora

Norah

Norbert

Noreen

Nori

Norma

Norman

Normand

Normandie

Norris

North

Norton

Norval

Norwood

Nour

Nova

Novah

Novalee

Novia

Noyce

Nuala

Nunatak

Nunzio

Nya

Nyah

Nyimbo

Nyla

Nylah

Nyle

Nyoka

Nyomi

Nyra

Nysa

Nyssa

O

Oak
Oaklee
Oakleigh
Oakley
Oaklyn
Oaklynn
Obadiah
Oberon
Obsession
Obsidian
Ocean
Oceana
Oceane
Oceanus
Octavia
Octavio
Oda
Ode
Odelia
Odessa
Odette
Odin
Odonata

Odyssey
Ofelia
Ogden
Oifa
Oilell
Oisin
Ola
Olaf
Oldrich
Olea
Oleana
Oleander
Oleg
Olga
Olin
Olive
Oliver
Olivia
Olivier
Olivine
Oliwier
Ollie
Olly
Olwen
Olwyn
Olympia
Olympus

Omar	Orlean
Omari	Orman
Omer	Ornelia
Omyra	Ornella
Onda	Orpheus
Ondine	Orquida
Onyx	Orrick
Oona	Orsa
Opal	Orson
Ophelia	Orville
Oprah	Osaka
Ora	Osbert
Orabela	Oscar
Oralie	Osckar
Oran	Osian
Orane	Osiris
Orange	Oskar
Orchid	Osker
Ore	Osman
Oren	Osmond
Oriana	Osvaldo
Oriel	Oswald
Orin	Oswin
Oriole	Othello
Orion	Otis
Orla	Otten
Orlando	Otter

Ottilie
Otto
Ouida
Ove
Ovid
Owain
Owais
Owen
Owin
Owyn
Oxford
Oyintsa
Oz
Ozette
Ozias

P

Pablo
Pacific
Pacifica
Packard
Paddy
Padraig
Paige
Paislee
Paisleigh
Paisley
Paityn
Paizlee
Palash
Palesa
Palma
Palmer
Paloma
Pamela
Pandora
Pangiota
Pangolin
Paniz
Panra

Pansy
Paola
Papatya
Paprika
Parhelion
Paris
Park
Parker
Parr
Parthenia
Parthenope
Pat
Patchouli
Patia
Patience
Patricia
Patrick
Patrik
Patrin
Patryk
Patten
Paul
Paula
Paulette
Paulina
Pauline
Paulo

Pavel

Pawel

Pax

Paxton

Payson

Payton

Payton / Peyton

Pazia

Peace

Peach

Peaches

Pearl

Pedro

Pell

Pema

Penarddun

Penelope

Penitentes

Penley

Penn

Penny

Penthia

Peony

Pepper

Percival

Percy

Peregrine

Peridot

Perla

Perre

Perry

Perry / Perrie

Persephone

Perseus

Pert

Perth

Petal

Pete

Peter

Petra

Petros

Petunia

Peyton

Phaedra

Phelan

Philemon

Philip

Philippa

Phillip

Philo

Phineas

Phoebe

Phoenix

Photinia

Phyllida
Phyllis
Phyllon
Pia
Picotee
Piera
Pierce
Pierre
Piers
Pierson
Pilar
Pilchard
Pine
Pinneped
Piotr
Pip
Piper
Pippa
Piran
Pixie
Placido
Plum
Poet
Polina
Polly
Poplar
Poppy

Popularaz
Porter
Portia
Posey
Posy
Powell
Prairie
Pranav
Precious
Prentice
Preslee
Presley
Preston
Primrose
Primula
Prince
Princess
Princeton
Priscila
Priscilla
Prisha
Priya
Promise
Prunella
Pryderi
Ptolemy
Putnam

Pwyll

Q

Qasim
Quaid
Quarry
Quartz
Qued
Queen
Queena
Queenie
Quennel
Quentin
Quill
Quin
Quince
Quincy
Quinn
Quinten
Quintin
Quinton

R

Rabbit
Rachael
Rachel
Rada
Radcliff
Radella
Rae
Raees
Raegan
Raelin
Raelyn
Raelynn
Rafael
Rafe
Rafferty
Rafflesia
Ragnar
Raheem
Rahul
Raiden
Raihan
Rain
Raina

Rainbow
Raine
Rainer
Rainey
Rainy
Raisa
Raizel
Raja
Rajan
Rajveer
Raleigh
Ralph
Ralphie
Ralphy
Ramiro
Ramon
Ramona
Ramsey
Randa
Randal
Randall
Randolph
Randy
Ranger
Rania
Ranier
Ransford

Ransley

Ransom

Ranveer

Raphael

Raquel

Rashad

Rasmus

Raul

Raven

Ravinger

Rawlins

Ray

Raya

Rayaan

Rayan

Rayburn

Rayden

Rayen

Rayhan

Raylan

Rayleen

Raylene

Raylynn

Raymond

Raymundo

Rayna

Rayne

Rayne / Rain

Rayyan

Raz

Read

Reagan

Reaghan

Reba

Rebeca

Rebecca

Rebekah

Rebel

Red

Redford

Reece

Reed

Reef

Reegan

Reese

Reeve

Regan

Reggie

Reghan

Regina

Reginald

Rehaan

Rehan

Reid

Reign
Reilly
Reina
Remi
Remington
Remy
Rémy
Ren
Renata
Rene
Rene / Renee
Renee
Renesmee
Reuben
Revel
Rex
Rey
Reya
Reyansh
Reyna
Reynaldo
Reynold
Rhea
Rhett
Rhiannon
Rhoda
Rhodes

Rhonda
Rhoswen
Rhyley
Rhys
Ria
Rian
Ricardo
Rice
Richard
Richie
Rick
Rickena
Rickey
Ricky
Rico
Rider
Ridge
Ridley
Ridwan
Rigby
Rigoberto
Rihanna
Riley
Riley / Ryley
Riley-james
Riley-jay
Rill

Rilla

Rilynn

Rina

Ringo

Rio

Riona

Ripley

Rishi

Rishley

Rita

River

Rivka

Rivulet

Riya

Rizwan

Roald

Roan

Robbie

Robert

Roberto

Robin

Robin/Robyn

Robyn

Rocco

Rochester

Rocio

Rock

Rockwell

Rocky

Roderick

Rodman

Rodney

Rodolfo

Rodrick

Rodrigo

Rogelio

Roger

Rogue

Rohan

Roise

Roisin

Roland

Rolando

Rolf

Rollie

Roma

Roman

Rome

Romeo

Romi

Romina

Romulus

Romy

Ron

Ronald	Rosemary
Ronan	Rosen
Ronat	Roshan
Ronin	Rosie
Ronnie	Roslyn
Ronny	Rosmarin
Rorey	Ross
Rory	Rosy
Rosa	Roux ('Roo')
Rosabella	Rowan
Rosalee	Rowen
Rosalia	Rowena
Rosalie	Rowyn
Rosalina	Roxana
Rosalind	Roxanna
Rosalinda	Roxanne
Rosalyn	Roxy
Rosalynn	Roy
Rosamel	Roya
Rosamund	Royal
Rosanna	Royalty
Rosario	Royce
Rose	Royston
Rosella	Ruben
Roselyn	Rubi
Roselynn	Rubina
Rosemarie	Ruby

Rudi
Rudolph
Rudy
Rudyard
Rue
Rueben
Rufus
Ruhi
Rumi
Rupert
Russell
Rusty
Ruth
Rutherford
Ryan
Ryann
Ryba
Ryder
Rye
Ryker
Rylan
Ryland
Rylee
Ryleigh
Ryley
Rylie
Rylin

S

Saad
Saanvi
Sabella
Sabina
Sabine
Sable
Sabrina
Sachin
Sacrifice
Sade
Sadie
Sadira
Safa
Saffron
Safwan
Sagar
Sage
Sahana
Sahara
Sahasra
Sahib
Sahil
Sai

Saif
Saige
Sailor
Saim
Saint
Saira
Saisha
Sakari
Sakura
Salem
Salil
Salix
Sally
Salma
Salman
Salome
Salton
Salvador
Salvatore
Sam
Sama
Samaira
Samantha
Samanvi
Samar
Samara
Samaya

Sameer
Sami
Samir
Samira
Samiyah
Sammy
Samphire
Samson
Samuel
Samuele
Sana
Sanaya
Sanders
Sandon
Sandra
Sandy
Sanford
Sanidine
Saniyah
Sanna
Sanne
Santana
Santiago
Santino
Santo
Santos
Sanvi

Saoirse
Saoloa
Sapphira
Sapphire
Sara
Sarah
Sarahi
Sarai
Saraid
Saray
Sargassum
Sariah
Sarina
Sariyah
Sascha
Sasha
Saskia
Sativola
Saul
Savanna
Savannah
Savina
Sawyer
Sayed
Saylor
Sayuri
Scarlet

Scarlett	Selma
Scarlette	Senan
Schuyler	Seneca
Scilti	Senna
Scoria	Sephora
Scott	Sequoia
Scottie	Sequoyah
Scotty	Serafina
Scout	Seraphina
Sea	Serena
Seabert	Serene
Seamus	Serenity
Sean	Sergio
Seanna	Serina
Season	Serval
Seb	Setanta
Sebastian	Seth
Sebastien	Seven
Sedona	Sevyn
Seerat	Seward
Sehaj	Shaan
Sekani	Shade
Selah	Shadow
Selby	Shadrack
Selena	Shae
Selene	Shaelyn
Selina	Shah

Shaila	Shell
Shaina	Shelley
Shale	Shepherd
Shanaya	Sheridan
Shane	Sherlock
Shanna	Sherlyn
Shannon	Sherman
Sharon	Sherpa
Shaula	Sherry
Shaun	Sherwood
Shauna	Shiloh
Shaurya	Shipley
Shaw	Shira
Shawn	Shirley
Shay	Shiv
Shayaan	Shona
Shayan	Shore
Shayla	Shoshana
Shayna	Shreya
Shayne	Shriya
Shea	Shyla
Sheena	Shylah
Sheikh	Sia
Sheila	Siana
Shela	Sibyl
Shelby	Sicily
Sheldon	Sid

Siddel
Sidney
Siena
Sienna
Sierra
Sigal
Sigmund
Silas
Silver
Silvia
Simeon
Simon
Simone
Simran
Sincere
Sinéad
Siobhan
Sion
Sipho
Sire
Sireli
Siren
Sirena
Siria
Sirius
Sitara
Siya

Skarlett
Skeet
Skipper
Sky
Sky/Skye
Skye
Skyla
Skylah
Skylar
Skyler
Skyler / Skylar
Slade
Slate
Sloan
Sloan / Slone
Sloane
Snow
Snowden
Snowdrop
Snowy
Socorro
Sofia
Sofie
Sojourner
Sol
Solana
Solange

Solaris
Soledad
Soleil
Solomon
Solstice
Solveig
Soma
Sona
Sonia
Sonja
Sonnie
Sonny
Sonora
Sonya
Sophia
Sophie
Sophronia
Sora
Soraya
Sorcha
Soren
Sorrel
Sparrow
Speck
Spencer
Spike
Spring

Spruce
Sri
Stacey
Stacy
Stanislaw
Stanley
Star
Starla
Starlight
Starling
Stefan
Steffan
Stella
Stephan
Stephanie
Stephany
Stephen
Stephon
Sterling
Sterling / Stirling
Sterne
Stetson
Steve
Steven
Stevie
Stewart
Stockard

Stokley
Stone
Storm
Stormy
Stratus
Strawberry
Stream
Stroud
Stuart
Studs
Sturgeon
Subhaan
Subhan
Success
Sufyan
Sugn
Suhani
Sulaiman
Sulayman
Sullivan
Summer
Summit
Sunny
Sunshine
Suri
Susan
Susana

Susanna
Susannah
Susie
Sutton
Suzanne
Suzette
Suzu
Svaty Vavrinec
Swain
Swan
Swara
Sycamore
Sydney
Sydney / Sidney
Syed
Sylas
Sylvan
Sylvester
Sylvia
Sylvie
Symphony
Szymon

134

T

Tabitha
Tadc
Tadeo
Tadhg
Taha
Tahlia
Tai
Taima
Taine
Taj
Tajsa
Takashi
Takoda
Tala
Talbot
Talha
Talia
Taliesin
Taliyah
Tallulah
Talon
Talya
Tamala

Tamar
Tamara
Tamarind
Tamarisk
Tamia
Tamir
Tammy
Tancy
Tanguy
Tania
Tanis
Tanner
Tansy
Tanvi
Tanya
Tao
Tara
Taran
Taras
Tarek
Tarian
Tariq
Tarn
Tarragon
Tarun
Taryn
Tatanka

Tate	Teithi
Tatiana	Temperance
Tatum	Tempest
Tatyana	Tenley
Taurean	Tennessee
Taurus	Tennyson
Tavares	Terence
Tave	Teresa
Tavish	Teri / Terry
Tavor	Terra
Tawny	Terran
Taya	Terrance
Taylan	Terrel
Taylen	Terrell
Taylor	Terrence
Tea	Terry
Teagan	Tesla
Teaghue	Tess
Teague	Tessa
Teal	Tetsu
Tecla	Tevin
Ted	Tex
Teddie	Texas
Teddy	Teyrnon
Teegan	Thabo
Tegan	Thaddeus
Tehile	Thais

Thalassa
Thalia
Thallo
Thandie
Thane
Thatcher
Thea
Thebe
Theirry
Thelonious
Theo
Theodora
Theodore
Theophile
Theresa
Thetis
Thiago
Thisbe
Thistle
Thomas
Thomasina
Thor
Thora
Thorn
Thorne
Thorpe
Thurlow

Thyme
Tia
Tiago
Tiana
Tianna
Tiara
Tiberius
Tibor
Tide
Tiernan
Tiernay
Tierney
Tiffany
Tigerlily
Tiggy
Tilly
Tim
Timber
Timmy
Timothy
Tina
Tinley
Tinsley
Tirzah
Titan
Titania
Titus

Tobias

Tobin

Toby

Toby / Tobey

Todd

Tom

Tomas

Tomasz

Tomkin

Tommie

Tommy

Tommy-lee

Tomos

Toni

Tonneau

Tony

Tony / Toni

Topaz

Tor

Tori

Torin

Torrey

Tory

Tory / Tori

Tostig

Townsend

Toyon

Trace

Tracy

Trahern

Tranter

Travis

Travon

Treasa

Treasure

Tree

Tremaine

Tremayne

Trent

Trenton

Treva

Trevon

Trevor

Trey

Trinity

Tripp

Tris

Trisha

Tristan

Tristen

Tristian

Tristin

Triston

Tristram

Triton
Triumphant
Trixie
Troy
Tru
Tru/True
Trudy
Truman
Trystan
Tuatara
Tucker
Tudor
Tulip
Tullia
Tunder
Tupelo
Turi
Turner
Turquoise
Twain
Twilight
Twyla
Ty
Tye
Tyler
Tyler-james
Tyler-jay

Tylor
Tymon
Tymoteusz
Tyne
Typhoon
Tyra
Tyree
Tyrell
Tyrese
Tyron
Tyrone
Tyson
Tzipporah

U

Uberto
Udath
Udaya
Udell
Udo
Ugo
Ula
Ulf
Ulises
Ulrich
Ulrika
Ultan
Ulysses
Uma
Umair
Umar
Umber
Umbra
Una
Undine
Unice
Unique
Unity

Unwyn
Upton
Urban
Urho
Uri
Uriah
Uriel
Uriela
Urien
Urja
Ursa
Ursula
Usher
Usman
Uta
Uttam
Uzair
Uzi

V

Vaclav
Vada
Vadim
Val
Valdemar
Valdis
Vale
Valencia
Valente
Valentin
Valentina
Valentine
Valentino
Valeria
Valerie
Valerio
Valery
Valia
Valkyrie
Valley
Van
Vana
Vance

Vandana
Vanellope
Vanessa
Vanetta
Vangelis
Vania
Vanity
Vanna
Vanya
Vaquita
Varda
Varden
Vardon
Varney
Varro
Varsha
Varun
Varvana
Vashti
Vaughan
Vaughn
Vavrin
Vavrinec
Vayda
Veda
Veer
Vega

Vela	Vianey
Velda	Vianna
Vella	Vianney
Velma	Vibol
Velvet	Vicenta
Venetia	Vicente
Venice	Vick
Venus	Vicky
Vera	Victor
Verbena	Victoria
Verda	Victory
Vered	Vicus
Verena	Vida
Verity	Vidal
Verna	Vidya
Vernell	Vienna
Verner	Vigdis
Vernon	Vihaan
Verona	Vijay
Veronica	Vikram
Versilius	Viktor
Veruca	Viktoria
Vesa	Ville
Vesper	Vina
Vesta	Vincent
Vester	Vincenzo
Vevina	Vine

Vinnie
Vinny
Viola
Violet
Violeta
Violett
Violetta
Violette
Virga
Virgil
Virgile
Virginia
Viridiana
Visara
Vita
Vito
Vittoria
Vittorio
Vitus
Viva
Vivaan
Viveca
Vivek
Vivian
Viviana
Vivianna
Vivianne

Vivien
Vivienne
Vladimir
Volker
Von
Vonda
Voss

W

Wade
Wakefield
Waldemar
Walden
Waldo
Waleed
Waleska
Walker
Wallace
Wallis
Wallis / Wallace
Walta
Walter
Walton
Wanda
Waneta
Ward
Wardell
Warner
Warren
Warwick
Washington
Wasim

Wassily
Watson
Wava
Waverley
Waverly
Wayland
Waylon
Wayne
Webster
Wednesday
Weldon
Wells
Wendell
Wendy
Werner
Werther
Wes
Wesley
Wesson
West
Westin
Westley
Weston
Wetherby
Weylin
Weylyn
Wharton

Wheaton	Willis
Wheeler	Willoughby
Whisper	Willow
Whit	Wilma
Whitfield	Wilmer
Whitley	Wilson
Whitman	Wilton
Whitney	Windsor
Wiktor	Windy
Wilber	Winifred
Wilbur	Winika
Wilda	Winn / Wynn
Wilder	Winnie
Wildflower	Winola
Wildon	Winslow
Wiley	Winston
Wilford	Winter
Wilfred	Winthrop
Wilfreda	Winton
Wilfredo	Wisdom
Wilhelm	Wistan
Wilhelmina	Wisteria
Wilkes	Wittan
Will	Wojciech
Willa	Wolf
William	Wolfe
Willie	Wolfgang

Wolfrom
Wolter
Woodburn
Woodrow
Woodward
Woody
Worcester
Worth
Wrasse
Wren
Wright
Wyatt
Wyclef
Wylie
Wynda
Wyndam
Wynn
Wynne
Wynnie
Wynter

X

Xadrian
Xanadu
Xander
Xannon
Xanthe
Xanthippe
Xanthus
Xaverie
Xavier
Xen
Xena
Xenon
Xerxes
Xeven
Ximena
Ximenna
Xiomara
Xiphia
Xiphosura
Xitlali
Xitlaly
Xiu
Xoan

Xochitl
Xoey
Xristina
Xylander
Xylia
Xzavier

Y

Yaal
Yadid
Yadiel
Yadira
Yadon
Yael
Yaelle
Yaffa
Yahaira
Yahir
Yaholo
Yahya
Yair
Yakiya
Yale
Yamila
Yamilet
Yamileth
Yana
Yaneli
Yangtze
Yanha
Yanira
Yanis
Yann
Yaqub
Yara
Yarden
Yareli
Yarely
Yaretzi
Yaretzy
Yaritza
Yarrow
Yaseen
Yash
Yasin
Yasir
Yasmeen
Yasmin
Yasmine
Yatzil
Yatziri
Yazmin
Ye
Yehuda
Yelena
Yeraldina
Yered
Yerik

Yerodin

Yervant

Yesenia

Yetta

Yeva

Yi

Yisroel

Yitzak

Ylva

Ynyr

Yobachi

Yogi

Yoki

Yolanda

Yoloti

Yona

York

Yosef

Yoselin

Yoselyn

Yoshiko

Yousef

Yousif

Yousuf

Yovela

Ysabel

Ysabella

Ysanne

Yseult

Yspaddaden

Yu

Yuki

Yuliana

Yulissa

Yuna

Yunus

Yurani

Yuri

Yuridia

Yuritzi

Yusef

Yusia

Yusra

Yusuf

Yuuta

Yuvraj

Yves

Yvette

Yvonne

Z

Zac
Zach
Zachariah
Zachary
Zachery
Zack
Zackary
Zackery
Zad
Zada
Zadie
Zadok
Zador
Zafar
Zafira
Zahara
Zahir
Zahra
Zaid
Zaida
Zaide
Zaiden
Zain
Zaina

Zainab
Zaine
Zaira
Zaire
Zak
Zakai
Zakaria
Zakariya
Zakariyya
Zakary
Zaki
Zaley
Zalie
Zamira
Zander
Zane
Zaneta
Zaniyah
Zara
Zarah
Zarek
Zaria
Zariah
Zariyah
Zavier
Zaya
Zayaan

Zayan	Zenaida
Zayd	Zendaya
Zayda	Zenevieva
Zayden	Zenith
Zayla	Zenobia
Zaylee	Zephyr
Zayn	Zeren
Zayna	Zeta
Zaynab	Zetta
Zayne	Zia
Zayra	Zikani
Zdenek	Zinaida
Zdenka	Zinerva
Zebedee	Zinnia
Zebulon	Zion
Zechariah	Zipporah
Zee	Zircon
Zeeshan	Zita
Zeina	Ziva
Zeke	Ziya
Zelda	Zoe
Zelenka	Zoey
Zelia	Zoie
Zella	Zola
Zelma	Zooey
Zemira	Zora
Zena	Zoraida

Zorina
Zosia
Zoya
Zula
Zuleika
Zulema
Zuleyka
Zulma
Zuma
Zumar
Zuri
Zuzana
Zuzu
Zyaire
Zyana
Zyanya
Zyla
Zyon

The   End

Manufactured by Amazon.ca
Bolton, ON